Modern Poetry

HERON LLOYD TAIT

Inks and Bindings
888-290-5218
www.inksandbindings.com
orders@inksandbindings.com
orders@booksidepress.com

This book is dedicated to my late mother, Sylvia Maud Tait. She gave me the start, which allowed me to acquire the wherewithal for accomplishing this work in the first place. Thanks to my children, Ron, Tanya, Kevin, Gillian, and Sabine. Their presence kept me going through very difficult times. Special thanks to Brenda for her moral support. Thanks also to Dr. Anthony Ronaldo Sebastian for his candor and belief.

Contents

OBSERVATIONS

SOCIAL

About Modern Poetry by the author

I believe that if you examined what Sir Herbert Edward Read said of Modern Poetry or Michelle L Devon's take on it you would get the tone and feel of my work in **Modern Poetry**.

Herbert Read said, "The modern poet has no essential alliance with regular schemes of any sorts. They reserve the right to adapt their rhythm to their mood, to modulate their metre as they progress. Far from seeking freedom and irresponsibility they seek a stricter discipline of exact concord of thought and feeling"

Michelle L Devon follows with "Modern poetry creates a short story with visual imagery, in a few lines rather than a few pages. Modern poetry touches your heart, by evoking emotions with which you can relate, about things you probably have experienced yourself.

The common themes for modern poetry are love and romance, nature, beauty, loss, and grief. These are all things that everyone can relate to, and when written in verse form with modern language use, a poem or piece of prose can bring out feelings long forgotten, remind of times of strong emotion, or speak of dreams for the future…all in a few lines instead of pages of story.

A good book or novel makes you think, striking the imagination… poetry and prose make you feel, striking the emotions. Why not give modern poetry a chance? You can search on line for samples or go to your local bookstore and pickup a copy and check it out. You may just be surprised how much you enjoy reading modern poetry!"

I hope my writings make for easy reading, enjoyment and emotional attachment to the themes.

SPIRITUAL

8

A Beautiful Prayer

May the beauty of the trees,
The birds, fruits,
And silence
Remind you of
The source of all goodness.

May the darkness
In your life
Give way to hope and fulfillment.

May the joys of achievement
Go tempered with
The serenity of humility
And the sorrow of losses
With the hopefulness of new beginnings.

May the wind of each song
Leave you with the
Echo of a desired
Refrain
And tunes of harmony,
With peace and happiness.

May each new day
Follow
Moonlights of
Passion, prayers, and praise.

May hopes for prosperity
Bring joys of
Achievement
And prayers through faith
The realization of dreams.

Our Condolence

We understand only
your expressions of loss
But we cannot know
the depth of your grief.
We understand that
with life comes sad parting,
But we know the stays
always seem brief.
Today as you think
and grieve for the loved one
That's gone ahead for
eternal sweet rest
We know, and with certainty
That his impartial promise
Brings knowledge secure
That he always knows best.

Perilous Paths

I see the way death lurks in the shadows
Angling to intercept the souls of the newly departed
Before they can go into the meadows
To be joined with the kindred and gentle hearted.
I can tell it knows these gentle people
Fashioned a life filled with good deeds
Eschewing the ways of the evil,
Bringing a harvest devoid of weeds.

I can tell by the look on its face
That it knows the difference between good and evil
That it insists on promoting every trace
Of the work of its captor, the devil
That it hopes to catch unawares
The pilgrims who took the long road
Knowing that their dreams, not their fears,
Would be realized as they focused the fold.

But as they cross the valleys
Of the shadow of death
Knowing that, as in the alleys
So in the cities, lies death's rancid breath
They struggled to avoid its traps
And to pass without falling into its pits
Relying on the knowledge that mishaps
Are to those whom the evil cap fits.

So they travel the narrow road to the end
Faithfully knowing with certainty that the gate
For which they fought, through faith, to enter
Would be ajar, completing their fate;
That, just as the choirs of angels promised
The misdeeds of the good are forgiven
They find the road they had chosen
Is the one that brought them their haven.

Give Me Everything

when my mind wonders
of life's whys
and wherefores
give me
understanding.

when my heart aches
from lack
of love lend
me your
breast.

when my
body wilts
from want of drink
lead me
to a stream.

when my eyes darken
from the scourge
of disbelief
give me
your light.

when my sinews ache
from this
hard journey
give me
thy balm.

when my resolve weakens
from the burden
of failures
give me
your strength.

when I am beset with doubts
and fears
lend me your
courage.

and
when I can bear no more
this load
give me
sweet and everlasting rest.

Wars II

Spars start wars
Stars man and arms,
Far away
And at all.

Tha fall,
Tha warmth,
Tha crystal days
Stall man and sat at bay.

Tha war last
All day and dark,
And far away
Tha war ran fat.

Aback and abaft
As tha sal car
Carry man and arms
Tha pass hard.

And man and arms
At afar
Land and start
And saw tha war.

All tha arms
At tha parts
That tha war was at
Adapt at arms.

Tha war saw many past
And all sad
That last tha war,
Ask all wars a ban.

Wars I

Small disputes cause wars
Fought by men with weapons,
In faraway lands
And everywhere.

Wars in the fall
In the summer
At wintertime
Keeping mankind in stasis.

Wars at daytime
Wars at nighttime
And everywhere
Wars grow in intensity.

Ships transporting armies
Though buffeted to and fro
Withstood aerial attacks
As they do storms.

But troops survived passage
And landed their weapons
Reinforcing
And joined in the fray.

Aircrafts and rockets,
Bombs and shells
Are severally deployed
Wherever wars are fought

Innocents killed as wars
Cause loss of friends,
And despite their bravery
Soldiers wish wars would end.

Wahn Biutiful Prayah

mi ope seh di beauti a di tree dem
ahn di bud dem, di frut dem ahn
quiatness
mek yu memba weh
ebri ting gud com fram

ahn mi ope seh di daak paat a yu life muuv
weh an mek ope ahn fulfilment riehn.

ope di hapines weh' yu mek supm' hapm
also mek yu memba fi
kip kaam ahn umble
ahn wen oonu hab sarro ar laas
memba seh ope ahn new staht dideh.

mi ope dat di sang dem weh yu sing
lef yu wid eko af the refrain weh yuh wahn
an tuunz af aarmoni
pees an hapines

ahn mi ope dat evri new dieh
com afta muunlitz
weh gi pashan, prayah ahn praiz

a ope dat yu wish fi praaspa
bring jai af acheevment an
prayaz af fait bring
di rializashan af dreemz

LOVE
AND
RELATIONSHIPS

A Morning Song

fair morning!
did you willfully bring
such sullen, sulky sky to my door;
forgetting to cause to cease the rain,
which would be better brought
to dampen, at springtime when
the grass is ready
to grace my garden,
the soil and moisten the grain?

and morning!
did you hope to bring
the wet, wintry winds to my pane;
forgetting to cause to cease
the cold,
which would be better wrought
to temper, at summertime
when the heat is ready
to take my breath,
the urge of my lung to fold?

and did, sweet morning,
you hope to cling
to the dark, dewy dusk of yesterday
not mindful that each new day,
or sun,
must overtake and replace
the spent force, the past,
and bring to bear
the hopefulness
of new beginnings and fun?

sweet morning!
you make me sing.
as nether noontime nears by minutes;
though might better be hurried by hours
to dusk,
when my love, nightfall,
will bring the chance, anew,
that slumber, tossing and dreams
may bring me, hopefully,
closer to her arms!

A Rare Find

treasures
are oft times
discovered
when not being
sought.

treasures come
oft times
unencumbered
with nary a
flaw.

Treasures are oft times disguised
as human beings.

treasures
are oft times
with monikers
as other items
especially, treasures, when
in the state and form
unique, as is each person.
they may not be discovered
even by all those that
surround them
day after day.

until,
voila!
quite by chance
does a stranger who just happened
to be in the right place, at the right time.
that is,
precisely,
how it came to be
that she found
her treasure, him,
serendipitously,
just in time,
last Christmas.

All for You

If I saw you crying, I'd cry too;
For I'd know, 'tis true,
My tears are of joy
If I cried with you.

If I saw you laughing, I'd laugh too;
For I'd know, 'tis true,
Your mirth summons joy
If I laughed with you.

If I saw you singing, I'd sing too;
For I'd know, 'tis true,
Our song is a love song
If I sang with you.

If I saw you dancing, I'd dance too;
For I'd know, 'tis true,
We'd dance to a love song
If I danced with you.

If I saw you falling, I'd fall too;
For I'd know, 'tis true,
I'd be falling in love
If I fell with you.

If I heard of your dying, I'd die too;
For I know, 'tis true,
Your dying would kill me
I'd have died with you.

If I cried with you, laughed with you, sang with you,
Danced with you, fell with you, and died with you;
My life would be complete,
I'd have found love with you.

Dream of Summer

Three hours we spent
Walking through the rain; Splashing
warm waters across the blades Not
caring for the grey day's lament.

Three hours we spent Singing
such wondrous tunes; The words
came easily to our lips
And then, meaningfully, they went.

Three hours we spent Savoring
sage, mint, and lime; Their
delicateness and potency
Rolled into one green scent.

Three hours we spent Gathering
bewitching flowers wild; So many
colors, so many fragrances
Portraying our life's sole intent.

Three hours we spent
Drinking nectar and mead;
The dizzying spells that were their grant
Rose as quickly as their descent.

Three hours we spent
Eating of lotus free; Euphoria and
sleep got intertwined With senses
of brew that ferment.

Three hours we spent Running
past wilting sheaves; Spoiling
for the day grown old
So we'd tarry alone in yonder tent.

Three hours we spent
Trying to make some sense;
Of the day gone so full yet so short
And of what this new dream all meant.

First Thoughts

the words, all six,
to which he surfaced
"good morning, love,
i got awake,"
were first proof
the heart beats,
the cortices respond.

wished his love
and him did he
on that new day
the best of life
as life can give.

her first meal,
he hoped, already down
and her resolve
to take on the world
now as palpable.

as for him, ablutions
complete, he
opened, would
make and take his
usual brew of nature's buds'
now homologous stew.

he'd hie about to impart
some clout to the world
he saw at once beautiful
as simple and simply
complicated.
aren't they lucky, opined he
to have part and share
of this piece of universe
where so diverse a product
of darwinian selection
did call home
whence the thought

of self may roam
as well, thoughts
that we be more
than some in
accomplishments
and deeds or, indeed,
less than some we may!

whichever!

enjoy the thoughts,
he wished her,
her dreams as well on
this day bestowed by
Him to them,
whether their perception
made Him or Her
man or mannequin,
or game or gnome
on this fertile, for thought,
complicated, unforgiving,
save by Him or Her,
particle of universe.

forsake the thought,
though, that being
be complete without
the complementary
being or thing ethereal.

his wish of her inclusion
of him in her thoughts that day
conceded the possibility that
this could be
the only contact,
one with the other,
made till then when the
traverse begins anew
of their fiery orb.

Indelible Love

whence the thought
that a simple entry on a chart
omitted, could undermine
what years of pain and sorrow
and ache and tears and fear
and hope and joy and happiness wrought,
even when time and space and
man conspire to imprison and
separate them from their love.
for if survival of their love did
in all these travails succeed
to strengthen their resolve,
to beat the ogres of envy and
hate and jealousy and curse
whence should the thought be
hatched that notation
of its start or the traverse
of their love to mark the march
of time be so powerful that
omission be poison for love's demise.
love owes no pay seeks
no credit nor price
nor interest but day by day
stands a shining pylon
that guides through maze
or haze or rain or gallows
and brings solace to the soul.
even in the end yet alive
does forge anew its bond
to join on the other side
of this bewildered land.

Looking for You

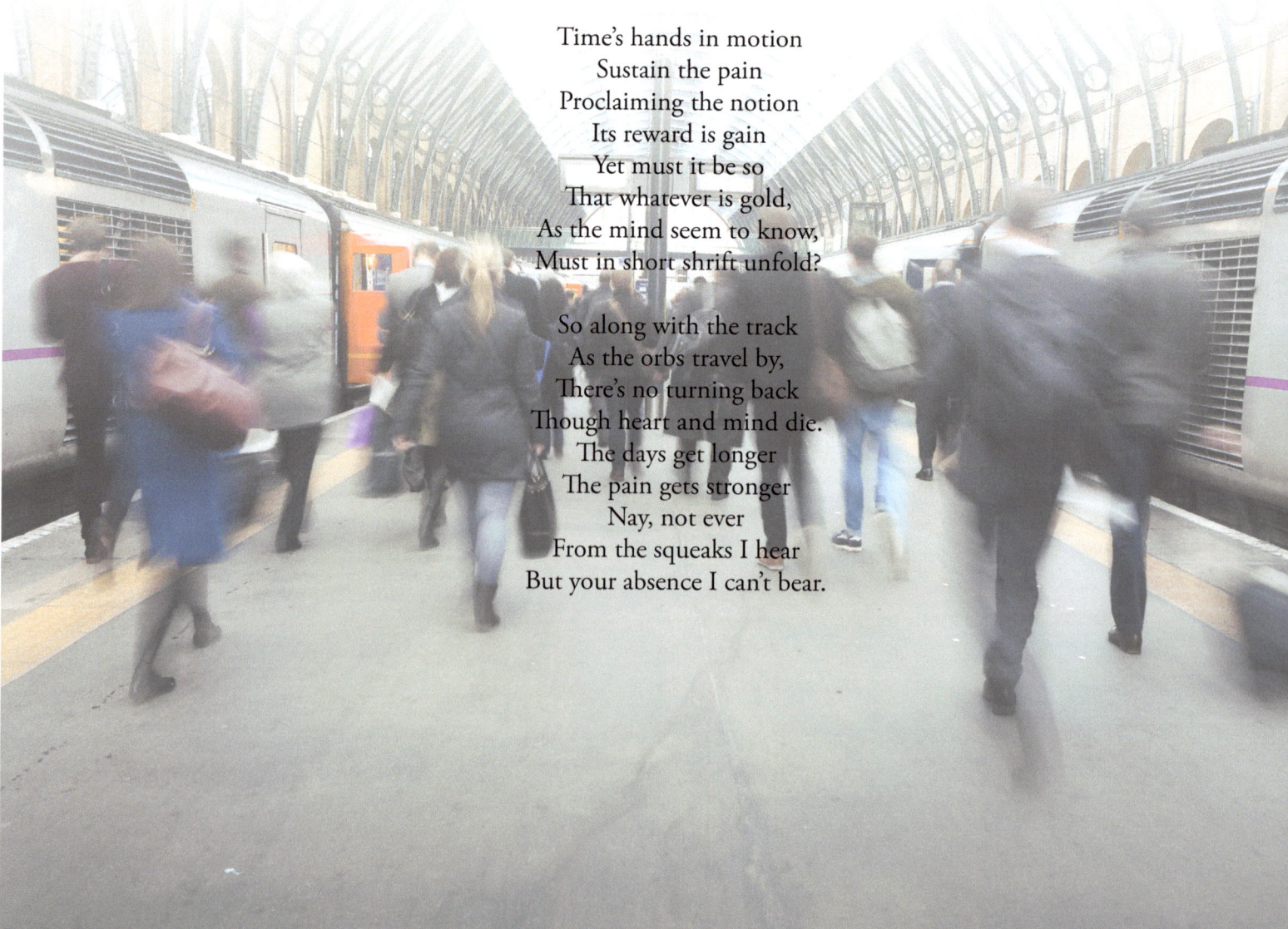

Back and forth
I drive the train;
The wheels squeak,
My heart burns in pain.
As I near the pier I
saw your form,
But stop after stop
It became the norm,
That each one I saw
And thought 'twas you
Turned out to be
No one I knew.

Time's hands in motion
Sustain the pain
Proclaiming the notion
Its reward is gain
Yet must it be so
That whatever is gold,
As the mind seem to know,
Must in short shrift unfold?

So along with the track
As the orbs travel by,
There's no turning back
Though heart and mind die.
The days get longer
The pain gets stronger
Nay, not ever
From the squeaks I hear
But your absence I can't bear.

I Love You!

I love you for your smile,
smile like a clear day
preceding many clear days,
bringing promise of a long
warm beautiful summer.

I love you for the sensible eyes,
eyes that light the way as we
go this treacherous life journey
a light of love and a guide
through perilous paths

I love your lips, lips to give
invite of the mouth perfect
with succulence and nectar
as lotus buds proffer their
elixir of potent aphrodisiacs
to spell the universe.

I love your enchanting voice,
voice speaking clear as violins with
potency in orchestra bold,
making the path to harmony setting my
heart to sing in tune the splash of
calm breaking waves
gurgling over the smooth pebbles.

I love your arms, slender arms that
bear our flags fluttering in the winds,
telling their changes flags of our spirits,
never ebbing flags proclaiming,
this is our ship, this is our space,
this is our port, this is our country,
this is our world, this is our universe,
this is our time.

I love your core, body whole of
feminine grace and purity whence
your issue proclaims proof of our love.
love that transcends words;
words with venom and hate,
love that overcomes trials and
tests to destroy,
love that slew demons of envy
and jealousy and pretense

I love your heart,
your golden heart that shines with
brilliance of kindness bestowed
upon those who seek to offer,
without counting the cost or
interest not sought in return.
heart that beats of harmony
of helpfulness that counts not
the time to show the way.

I love your story, story that
bespeaks of modesty with truth
of humble means, retiring desires,
without regard to pride or to
concealment of the past,
where courage and pride of purpose
overcame all odds to succeed.

All these loves and yet
I love you most for the beauties
I cannot describe,
beauties recorded on my mind whence
my love springs eternal
over time, over space over hope,
and over faith.

Let Our Light Shine

I preened your skin showed
my love from within and
when there is doubt
i left all negatives out.

I spoke all kind words
e'en when i could shout
i unruffled your feathers
when you under the weather.

The tall tales that you tell
i parried very well
and when you are made sad
happy stories i tell.

Like a doctor of life
i did with such ease
whatever things ail you
i cured the disease.

Your kin folks I treat with
such feathery heat when
you stumble and call
i steady your feet.

Yet methinks all the time
as I'm told many moons past
hosts of deed that's been done
bear no force 'less it's the last.

So i've resolved myself a way
which I'll carry out with élan
that we each need full degree
to complete our life's plan.

Henceforth then I say,
for your sake and mine
each's mission's a hundred percent
to keep our life light ashine.

Memory of Her

If you could know
The joy that it brings
When she unveils
Her matchless charm!
She will not harm
Either flesh or mind
As deep within
Dwells a heart that's kind.
At the seaside at times
When the tide,
Neap beside
The drifting tryst,
The blue cover ever high,
The searing disc beating down,
An unwilling frown
Or childlike sigh
Did promote;
She, without thought
Of self, or heat,
Or scorching feet,
Tarried at his side
While they drifted
Into where, once,
The horizon abide.
If you could know
The joy in her sharing
Neither seeking nor caring
Of same measure denied,
Of unbalance implied:
Sated by the high
Of the pleasing,
And with clarity of love
For the beau
All wishes appeasing;
Ever would you know
An emotion, mature
From the dawn
In the meeting,
Through to twilight, depleting
Her universe
For him,
Till the end.

Memory of You

I saw the sun depart into the hills
Sensing too well the end of the thrills
That filled the day like a goblet, into which
Memories of you will forever be stored.
Like good wine, they only get better
As daydreams pass and make it matter
That drop after perpetual drop fills my mind
With the wish and urging of them to be poured.

I saw the sun depart into the hills
Willing the birds ready to roost, their shrills
Etching an enchanting aria on the mind; a song that
Imprints your voice, always in tune.
That warm, softly euphoric feeling
Swings me to a zenith far exceeding
The bronzed hills, which our tryst did hide,
Where forever memories of you will abide.

I saw the sun depart into the hills
Now alone, peering down to my window sills,
Alone, except with ambivalence of sadness and joy,
I recounted the power of your laughter.
Power that translates it to three words never said,
Power to wish you back with me instead
And as the time to pass till then starts anew
Memory of you will make the days seem few.

My Valentine

lady love!
you looked into me,
stared at my soul
and artfully ingrained
the essence of your being,
a wondrous mystery
for all to behold,
and feel, and crave,
like i crave
for her.

but
i am blessed,
i believe. yes!
for many hanker
for that which you planted
making me whole
to the depths
of my soul.

the bounties
of your treasure
promise
to glow to the end of time,
to welcome,
to tease
forever.

alas! for
i live
cursed
too.

as my taut senses
detect same raw power
through which you
endowed her,
tantalizing
me into a whirlpool
of charm, fomenting
magma searing
within.

yet,
you forestall her
sojourn into the
thickness
of the throng
that yearns
your
lusted implant,
lest my desire
should contrive
to grasp
the complement
for my molded id.

forever
i shall try,
and my curse
will last;
for my will does match well
the degree of its sting
giving them life
a million moons,
even
till i die.

Vicarious Love

The words you used to describe her love
Left no uncertainty on earth or above;
Of the depth of passion to which you did go
Sparing not of danger or emotion that flow.

I think of our love and know it true
No day has passed that I have ever been blue;
No word you have said or act you commit
Could elicit one tear or a rage or a fit.

Yet, seems to be that the past be now
You wear his loss on your furrowed brow;
You gave me yours which
I know to be real
Though a bit of retention is part of the deal.

We passed many days in the hills and the dales
The zephyrs we welcome and buffet the gales;
The flowers we picked were perfect to my sight
Yet to you one more brush stroke would make nature right.

I ponder the ways
I could make the best
Of the love I will give as we fashion our nest;
Now I am convinced of a promise I'll keep
Of the gift I should offer to make perfect our sleep.

As the warm days progress and long nights beckon
For the good of our hearts forever this I reckon;
For now and always to this I agree
Let your thought be of him as you lie here with me.

You Made Me You

i wandered the land
without the loving hand
i could hold, to guide
me to her trusting side;
near of the one i see as mine.
the days got meaner,
yet my nays multiplied as each
my mind did tell,
was but a barren trace and
not the place where i could grow.
i wandered this land and,
in a sense knew
some years now spent,
that the hand i found
would belong to you.
how beautiful then
that you made me special!
you made me special
when you said your words,
your three words
with your charming silence.
you made me special
when you showed your eye.
you made me special
when you gave your first smile.
you made me special
when you came with me.
you made me special
when you believed in me.
you made me special
when you trusted me.
then i made you special
when you made me you.

Complement

see autumn trees;
goldens, reds,

complementary.

no closer can
they get
unless they
learn from us.
we are
the ultimate;
standing
as two
yet together
unitary.

complementary.

the sun, the moon
boiling, cool;

complementary.

no closer can
they get
unless they
meld like us.

we are the ultimate.

temperaments,
temperatures.
fiery, staid.

together,
warm.

complementary.

Spoiled

she elicited loud laughter
and with pleasant
surprise.
it were said well
if this were her wont
day by day,
as it builds his yearn
for the tenderness
of her touch;
touch of an enchanted
berry on bewitched lips;
the sweet golden of
her voice like
a heavenly harp,
under the spell
and wizardry of
a gentle gnome.
he thinks it a miracle
that on that morn
she should him
so pleasantly surprise.
she spoiled him then
by that sweet act:
warm nectar dripping
to an orchid's lair,
making him foolishly
await its repeat,
as each new sun fidgets,
tantalizingly, with
the clouds scurrying up:
seemingly seeking
to make for them
a fleecy cushion
where they can, again,
safely ensconce
in each others' arms.

Nature and You

see the scenery,
calm, composite of many hues:
the main protagonists trees,
shrubbery
serene sky, and babbling water.
they make an acceptable, no . . .
they make a workable band.
the trees I think are symbolic of you,
stoic, well rooted and seemingly
leaning towards the water.
the symbolism . . . always on the
move yet always there
complementing,
whatever scene.
yonder sky completes
the dynamism of the picture . . .
portraying the heavens
which lend a spiritual imperative
guarding and protecting
and keeping us together,
a mélange insuperable.
perfection is a concept
and we may strive towards but
must remain ever cognizant of
its improbability as
we try to make harmony
with the universe even
as we try to define,
find and timidly seize it.
what is sure, and this I know
that harmony is fleeting that
love so untouchable,
indestructible, intractable
even separated by time
and space and thought,
will remain etched
most indelibly
upon the memory.

OF PLACES
AND TIMES

Beds

the beds made
and populated
with roses and asters and
zinnias are just that . . . beds. made once,
but dug many times and cultivated
and mulched with leaves and twigs and waste
of cows and mules,

(maybe they were donkeys,
but certainly not horses,
for those were rare in those
parts in those days)

and goats and even,
at times, fowls.
beds for roses and, as said,
beds for asters and zinnias too;
zinnias the size of hibiscus
that formed the edge;
the hedge of hibiscus,
pruned and shaped
as straight as his crooked
cutlass would allow

(OK, a bad workman quarrels with his tool)

hibiscus in bloom:
red and pistilled
and stamened
and colored.
with hummingbirds
flitting around.
but, aah, yes, the beds of roses,
of asters, for which came praise,
and zinnias;
praise from mister linton,
for these zinnias (wonder if he remembers)
beds all perfectly square
and watered twice daily,
after six, ere bamboo's heat or darkness
would descend. perfectly

straight, those beds, (except where the land
that formed the boundary
between reggie's

and vernon's acres,
or half that,
petered to a point . . .
straight nonetheless)
and the roses and asters
and zinnias as big as hibiscus
blooming from the hedge
that marks the edge
of the plot of land
that held the cottage,

(as so sometimes called by reggie,
name was reginald, the boy's father,
though all were wont to call him reggie)

the family home really,
where lived five girls
and the boy who made
the beds for roses and asters
and zinnias and, yes, yes, marigolds,
those with yellow buttonlike devices,
beckoning the honeybees

(for there were many hives in that area of
saint ann, jamaica, one thousand nine
hundred and fifty-nine when the beds came
into being, actually he, the boy, made them)

and the wasps

(i sometimes wondered why they
bothered: they don't make honey)

the beds kept the roses
and asters and zinnias
and marigolds
supremely comfortable
as they prospered
and grew as large as
Hibiscus elatus.
there was, of course,
the mother and there was the father
and there were those five girls and
the boy. he alone

(well, he would call on the sisters for
help with gathering the manure
from the hillside,
their own little col,
affectionately called hillcrest)

made the beds,
and cut the wood,
and milk the cows,

(imagine getting out of bed at four in the
morning and walking two, maybe three miles;
though it seemed like ten then.
he soon enjoyed dawdling, dragging his bare feet
through the dewy grass, forgetting that
he had to complete his chore
and take his father's breakfast to hilltop,
the name of the prison where
he worked as a prison officer)

and collect the manure;
because he wanted
to make the beds
as comfortable as could be for
those beauties that stayed,
immobile, lucky, nothing-to-do in them.
yes, they swayed
and gaily waved their
heads as the wind
blew in from the north east;

(probably the remnants of the northeast
trade winds that deposited their moisture
on the other side of the hills. sometimes cold winds
. . . we were told they came from canada. imagine!
all the way from canada, second largest country
in the whole world; fancy that)

but that was all they ever did,
except grow so well.

the boy made the beds.
just as the man, today,
made this bed;
just this time with bed linen . . .
linen of cotton and silk,
and fleece, though

not of sheep, just of man's devices;

(but only one bed
for he now sleeps alone)

but fleece nonetheless;
soft and more fluffy,
much more fluffy than
the mulch and droppings of goats
and donkeys and cows,
that foraged on the grass nearby,
and the corn leaves also
drenched with brew of hops
and milk and eggs
for that special bull.

he caused fears to all six
but never once
did he disturb the beds
made for the roses
and asters and zinnias and marigolds.
yet this new bed with
so expensive a garb and with
no unpleasant smells
of dung of donkeys, and cows,
will not give, every time, the comfort
that they got, those lucky roses,
and asters and zinnias
and marigolds, that he may
sleep and not lay awake
pondering the beds
made those summer days
in saint ann, jamaica,
in the year one thousand nine
hundred and fifty nine
when he had barely a dozen.
those beds that gave comfort
to the roses and asters
and zinnias and marigolds
and, how could i forget, carnations.
it cannot be the fault
of the bed . . . the bed
made with soft cotton,
linen and pumped
with air to that number
that should be comfortable for him,
as comfort and praise,

and beautiful blooms
came for those roses
and asters and zinnias
and marigolds and carnations and,
now and then, snapdragons.

now he, grown and now
not employing mulch
and dung and leaves
and shrubs for the bed, his bed.

he knows that it is comfortable
for he made it with the same
pride and care and neatness
and fluffy and comfortable,
and most night he sleeps
like a baby.
but on those days when
disturbed his calm forgets nothing,
especially the unfair
and dishonest and untrue or
half true and the beds of roses and asters
and zinnias and marigolds
and carnations and snapdragons.
wish that he could be like them.
they with no thoughts

(or so he thinks)

not of fleece or of cotton nor of
the bed nor of unnecessary
words in his head.
even coming close to wishing dead!
but conclude should
wish only for peace,
and calm, and sunshine and rain,
and now computers,

and digital tuners . . .
modern timers . . .
and sometimes, snow, like on december 24
ere the dawn of december 25.

(for he is now way, way up;
up there from whence, he was told,
came those trade winds.
did not know if it was true at the time)

and truth.

no praise required
just love and close, real close!
for the man who made
the comfortable beds
for the roses,
for the asters,
for the zinnias,
for the carnations,
for the marigolds,
for the snapdragons and with these new
modern beds of fine linen for him,

and

for all those who forget that in better
times he made and feathered their beds.

comfortable beds.

Causeway Road

Not particularly wide
It carries vehicles of all sorts.
You cannot miss the trams
As they obey those parallel
Or concentric snakes,
Emitting their squeaky laments.

Then the double-deckers.

Beautifully scraping façades
Of toothpick edifices;
Dozing patrons oblivious
Of their fortune, their soft
Cushy saddles, as possessed
By these iron British horses.

Double-decks, singles
Mini of sixteen seats
Trams, seemingly ready
To capsize, and taxis
Scooting the length
Three, four, five,
Sometimes six abreast
And width of well traveled
Hong Kong's Causeway Road.

Christmas Shopping

Why would you think
of Christmas shopping
at this time of year
with summer still to spend
and autumn in the tow
gifting yet months to go?

you promised, I know, to send
your friends all bought items in
stores from their
old countries and more.
well, you could start by
going to **africa**
for the kente cloth
you promised tamar your **ghana**ian friend
you can most likely find some
in maxmart or shoprite.

it won't be hard to find
the **kitenge** in nakumatt
for fatima and
adele would sure like a **sifsari**
which you could pick up
a good price in carrefour.
(OK, I know . . . price is of no concern)
imagine your waltzing into **casablanca**
kaftans for joe and tom you
are sure to find the buba you
promised bola in the mega plaza.

woolworths and **stuttafords** are
probably not good places
to find an izincu but a local
zulu department store will
show the way for you.
woolworth still trades
in **tanzania**
but you may not find
a khanga there for tess but
uchimi is just the place
could be your saving grace.
you won't need to shop in **canada** or **usa**
before november, but in central
and south america
you could blaze a trail there now.

from el palacio de hierro and sansborn
in **mexico** and **guatemala** respectively
la reina in **puerto rico**
and dante in **panama**
any gift there is fine.

the trek thru america del sur
into jumbo in **argentina** and
north into **chile** for jumbo
or corona.
eta fashion in **ecuador** and
ripley in **peru** will help.
ketal and daslu in **bolivia**
daslu in **brazil** as well.

almas in **bangladesh** will provide
alternatively meena bazaar
china's boasts beijing hualian.

hong kong has european stores
and sogo should serve well.
indian fashions at debenhams
star bazaar or **brampton** shops
all carry garbs for shams.

indonesia stores matahari
daiso or alun alun
iran's ssmart, and hamee will
serve quick for turnaround
israel's hamashbir lazarchan
(since shekem has closed down)
while **pakistan** premier store
may come from makro,
imtiaz and pace in central **lahore**.

philippines adora and gaisano
tiong san or robinson's
will get you what you seek
saudi arabia's bin dawood and debenhams
are great from week to week.
Seek out mustafa and
company in
singapore
as well as is daiso.
south korean jeonju core

and hyundai department store
carry all you want and more.

taiwan's pacific sogo and talee
thailand's hat yai
pata in **bangkok** should serve
both for gifts and culinary fare.

in **dubai**, **uae** harvey nichols,
geant and centrepoint
vietnam's tax vincon
and eden mall will prove
up to the task for all
that group of friends.

lebanon has aishti and city mall.
austria has interspar
azerbaijan park bulvar
and port **baku**
are perfect before nightfall.

the **czech republic** has kotva
cyprus debenhams, marks & spencer.
while anttila in **estonia** and **finland**
provides feast for the shopping eyes
before dinner.

You may want to walk
The streets for illum
in **denmark**'s swanky streets.
la samaritaine and printemps for **france**,
you know their great eats.

germany has ahrens in marburg
kadewe in **berlin** and
carsch-haus in **dusseldorf.**
latvia top rimi
makes for a
splendid sign-off.
italy has coin and la rinascente
ireland arnotts and clerys
while hagkaup in **iceland** fokas
in **greece**
lithuania's europa
should make your european tour brief.

luxembourg's monopol

holland's de bijenkorf and hema
should make for a quick oass
to **norway**'s steen & strom
and **poland**'s galleria central
portugal and spain sport
el corte ingles
russia with apraksin dvor and stockmann
serbia with robne kuce beograd
makes marks & spencer
superfluous as does
slovenia's tus makes marcatur.

sweden ahlens and gekas
could be skipped for
the common sense store here
whilst **switzerland** with globus and loeb
should spice you shopping fare.

turkey sports beyman and ykm
marks & spencer
the omnipotent
is a good place to
say bye for home.

before that though
take a long ride to **australia**
how about kmart, target we
see them in our town
david jones my be the aussie
to send you on your own
author barnett and farmers
in **new zealand**
should finally see you through
the shopping and you head
to your homeland.

'twas four months you departed
to test your vigor for shopping
the packages you sent
will make a philatelist
hopping.

the deal you made
is surely fulfilled
the shopping you started for
christmas is done before the
season has started.

Sunset Negril

she stood
on the craggy cliff
contemplating
the arrival of
the evening
sun.

its chariots,
drawn
by troikas and tandems
preceded
with the lights
of a thousand
stars.

each horse
chortling in
with eyes the reflection
of polished
diamonds,
cut their most brilliant finish.

the bridles
were fashioned
of ropes
wrought with
wispy clouds,
labor of navvies
toiling
through the noonday sun.

she wondered
of the heat
and sunburn
they must have suffered
in the ovens
of the jamaican
summer.

yet as she eyed the scene,
scantily clad subjects showed
no sign of fatigue or scorch

or blister or thirst,
having been soothed by
the prevailing winds
spraying
their refreshing power,
a thousand showers
of fluvial mists.

the winds
subsided as the
whole atmosphere
became bewitched
with an eerie calm.

then the drivers with a
lash of their whips
gurgled an almost
imperceptible yodel
that signaled
the enchanted steeds
to train their eyes
on the evening sunshine,
simultaneously throwing
a fiendish snort
that scattered their rays onto
the yonder horizon,
effecting a glorious
kaleidoscope across
the western sky.

the display survived for a
quarter of a turn whilst
those alive nearby,
touched by the magnetism
joined her in marveling
at its ecstatic beauty,
fading softly
into the negril
twilight

PHILOSOPHICAL

Dilemma of Man

How can you ask a tree,
Sated with the elixir of life,
Shrouded in golden sunshine,
And rooted to the bosom of nature,
To not flaunt its wonderful plumage,
To not produce its treacherous bounty,
To not withstand the swirling gusts,
Nor enhance with each season its girth!

How can you ask a baby,
Ensconced in the arms of its mother,
Nourished with goodness of colostrums,
Luxuriating in warmth of its swaddling,
To not purr and coo and gurgle,
To not babble in tongues of the ether,
To not reward its lifeline with warm smiles,
Nor crave the cuddling before sleep!

How can you expect the farmer,
Having chosen good, vibrant seed,
Tilled and furrowed and mulched,
Researched, consulted, and prayed,
To not expect bountiful harvest,
To not hold proffer of sustenance,
To the offspring and to the partner,
Or to himself for the cycle to repeat!

How can you expect the Man,
Wired by nature his mate to complement,
To not follow the mandates of his programs,
To control the senses even as enter,
Activates each by the opposite that attracts,
To fulfill the mandates of his race,
Whose participants must record win or dead heat,
If the hands of extinction they must defeat!

Disillusion

Two-thousand moons long passed
That had the dawn
The bridge and the twilight
In quick succession drawn.
What ecstasy the difference
The mind surmised should unfold!
Yet dawn to night giving deference
Unwrapped a rift, a chasm bold
Once the tide of light
Time's hands put to flight.
A torrent of emotion brew
In laughter, in chatter as grew
The bloom, the promise, the mark
To nurture into night, till the dark
To cherish day-to-day.
But promises fade away
Matured in measure short
And fulfillments abort.
The mind did say
To quench the pride
The hurt to hide
It may be wise
To hurry his demise.
For if love is pain
Then death is gain
And solace not to find
Where promise, unkept
And care bereft
Of where two selves did bind.
Nor tarry he must
As nothing, save dust
From whence they were pressed
Remains arrest.
Some thousand moons long passed
The dream came hither in time to wither
And fly on wings
Of unseen beings
In the ether.

I Believe

i believe in the universe,
love, hate, and forgiveness;
that love resides on the other side
of the coin to which hate is borne.
i believe that the universe balances the coin delicately,
yet allowing its subjects,
when, or if, they chose to dig, inwardly,
from the perspective that they occupy
to find the coin, despite thickness,
easily penetrable, to the core,
wherein forgiveness abides.

i believe in happiness,
wrath, kindness, and peace
that they abide in close proximity to,
and ruled by the heart, the mind, and the soul.
i believe that the palpable, as they cease,
exhort and beseech of the universe,
happiness, kindness, and peace
for mind and soul

and i believe the soul
tarries with the universe insuperable,
indestructible, by time and space, over millennia
to appear and traverse, anew, with vigor, pride, and purpose,
through boundaries of body, heart, and mind
to know love, hate, forgiveness, happiness,
wrath, kindness, and peace

i believe in me

I Don't Know

If asked for your thought
Of the car that I bought,
Or the road best to take
So we may not arrive late,
You soon answer, "I don't know!"
Yet, would it be accurate,
As I am wont to suggest,
That you kept the thought
In exchange for the surrogate?
Does the use of that tact
Serve to hide the fact
Of unwillingness to seem
Foolish or wise or unsure of
Your pride or self-esteem?

Your favorite flower
May be mine or the drink.
You may feel just as right
At the ballpark as the rink
Yet you say, "I don't know!"
Let's me think in a trice
That the thought of the play
On trimmed grass or on ice
May be right any day.

But a fear that to make
Decisions or partake
Of the blame for a day
Spent in unfulfilling play
Will return to your mind
If I am critical or unkind.

Take a stand bold and free
Even if no one agrees
Your thoughts are as valid
And right and useful
As one can give rise
To another and the prize.

And at the end of the day
You can with pride say
I gave it my all
"I don't know" is displaced
Self-esteem is well laced.

Make Your Day

accept yourself
the way you are
and stand secure
that you love the one
you see in you.
love yourself
and hope not to
find what others
want of you
but what lies there
for your mind to see.
search yourself
and, finding no fault,
accept yourself
perfect for you.
for that perfection
lies in your imperfection;
as being human
implies imperfection.
therefore life is full
if, in the end,
you accept the id
you find in you.
then, and only then,
can you be sure
that you can have
the one true love,
the one you accept exists.
so let him only express a love,
who accepts the truths
of what you are,
who you are,
why you are
a perfect human

with all his
imperfections;
those that you
find in you,
or the ones
not seen but
known must reside.
for in the end,
all declarations
of love remain
but for the instance
that you please.
they remain selfish love,
love of self:
not as you
love yourself,
and always will be,
but as he finds you
for the moment.
such expression, then,
comes as your deeds
are acceptable
for the purpose to be
fulfilled at the moment
and not for you
the person you are,
always residing there.
you may accept
then you may
not as you are free
to feel the love for you or
the love from the deed.
ultimately,
you make your day
as you reflect
yourself not by the deed
but by your being.

Trees

They start at creation, grew from seeds
Rearrange sun and chlorophyll for our needs
Each sprung with a purpose
Even measuring the right dose
So it's antidote for other's poisonous deeds

Though small one may grow from large stone
Really large one from small acorn alone
Eat its fruit from The Garden
Did Eve and Adam without pardon
Since the snake wanted path to the throne

Those trunks are not used to store clothes
Rings across tell of annual throes
Even though they'd been xylem
Eons pass and did harden them
Surely these cells won't imprison hoboes

Their tissues sometimes crushed for paper
Reforestation not burning is safer
Every one they replace
Ended up in some race
So the winner be richer and baser

Thousand eons and even more pressure
Reacted for black tarry issue
Every land that possesses it
Engender serious cash deposit
Some, like Iraq, got wars: Iran censure.

Take the time and go hug-a-tree
Reactionary and activists agree
Every one that we save
Even if it points us the grave
Could uphold this human pedigree

Solitude

morning coffee,
birds, songs of birds.
could swear i hear
their words stream,
babbling!

after nine hours. and dream.
wide-eyed maybe at five and the best is
a hundred paragraphs.
written, not read . . . yet.
of trees, of squirrels,
of ducks. paragraphs for kids.
like max, like layla.
like sophia.

no words to translate,
save mine; none to decipher,
underestimate no words for sorry.
for misunderstand, for no-reply,
for too-much-answer-back.
no intimate. only sounds.
sounds i make . . . listen!

sounds of trees, and sights.
sounds of colors.
green greens, yellow greens,
greenish yellows.
all make the same sound.

mellowed cones.
quiet barks . . . of trees.
these . . . oak, . . . elm, . . . ash.
i name, they agree
they accept my names.
they accept my clothes,
of lack thereof;
even as the bed accept
my birth clothes,
like found-ins
on nudist beach,
in a turkish bath.
(did i take a bath?)
skip it!
no knowledge, my bed, of it;

of nude, of mood,
and care less of breasts,
of thighs, of pubic hair of
moans, of sighs.

that . . . i find,
to be precise,
quite fair.

no explanations for sounds,
nor for prayers. (did i pray?)
no contradictions,
no makeup,
no made up reasons.
no excuses, no sulk.

and, corn porridge is fine.
no whine for no-wine suppertime.
porridge is fine at breakfast or lunch.
and no-steak dinnertime.

no mouthwash,
no worry of what I ate
or did not, no car, no horns....
no horns for release.
so i unpack my bags and know it's . . .
not yet. not now.
(who needs them?)

the roads, the cars the noise,
the people. government.
no! not yet.

just not ready
for that. for money!
credit cards!
smoke! toke! tokens.

just rest. sweet rest. i must maintain
sweet, quiet, carefree, comfortable,
rest. i am well rested. but,
i must prolong . . . . this!

this solitude!

Things to Love

Expansive blue sky reigning high
Comfort preceding fulfillments' sigh
Warm, westerly, winter winds
Are some of my treasured favorite things
Never mind the time of day
'Tis always fun to hear kids at play
Never mind the place I live
I've always found 'tis win to give.

Pineapples, peaches, pears, cherries
Passions, papayas, plums, raspberries;
Buds of mums and frocks of nuns,
And hives of bees and pollen and puns
Never mind the time of day
'Tis always cool to stop and pray
Never mind the place I travel
Architects never fail to marvel

Croissant, cabbage, crouton, pies
Carrots, callaloo, cinnamon, fries:
Cream of wheat and racks of lamb,
And kegs of wine and roasts of ham
Never mind the time of day
'Tis always soon to hear mom say
"Time to play and time to weep,
But now, my son, 'tis time to sleep"

Audi, Lexus, Bentley, Benz,
Can never take the place of friends.
Wool and linen and silk and leather
Carry as much weight as a feather.
But, never mind the time of day
You'll now and always hear me say
Massage the plasma to a boil
The fitting end to a long day's toil.

EXPERIENCES

Counting Sheep

can clearly recall
when
sleep came so easily
as easily as the air recedes
from between the weary
head and the worn linen.

the rain came sometimes
and the pitter-patter
morphed
into henpecking on the corrugated
metal.

finally that thunderous din
that soothed the sinews
the mind
and the heart
but mostly there was calm
except for the cicadas
and
the croaking of frogs or toads
and crickets and owls and
intermittent yaps of mongrels
solidifying
their next day's morsel.

but sleep did come
sans
count of sheep or wonder why not.
there was no reason to wonder
why not
with all the organic citrus
and carrots and mangoes and
tomatoes and apples and corn
and cabbages
as big as carriages
and yams.

tastes heavenly.
we still have yams and cabbages
all bigger than carriages
engineered

as are the carrots
and apples and shriveled citrus
and huge nonorganic strawberries
not mulched with straws.

only
reflecting monsanto's revenge.

no wonder
we now lie awake
griping from the scourge of all
engineered
fruits and vegetables
and trans-fat and sulphites and
aspartame and plastics and cholesterol
and pollution and margarine.

(can't believe it's not glorious butter)

and no sugar
and caffeine and tv dinners
and seinfeld and news and radiation
that keeps the ears buzzing.

clearly
we can't recall when
we did get twenty-eight thousand
seconds of zees.

but
we know that we stay up nights
wondering why sleep
will not upon our weary bodies
descend
as we count leaping sheep.

Charade

she called him friend
he did believe
but her mind
was set
on lofty goals that
formed beliefs in
her for him.
she gave her all
and he did fall
for all the deeds and

smiles and treats.
she did not skip a beat as
he sang her praise . . .
'twas all angelic
the way
she got things done.

time and space and
strength and grace
were ne'er in short of place.
the years now the past
did not outlast
her vigor and her vim as
she showed both child and
superwoman with tenacity
and guile and grin.

she smiled
when things were good seemed
sad when his fortunes fade.
none on this orb could ever
sustain a more royal
and pretty charade.

but there were perilous underflows
turbulence that if he did know were
swirling 'neath his feet
would understand and surely
intercede to parry her well planned beat.

the friends he kept
were never right
never fine enough for him or bright.
though he'd shown

he had no thought
of being their
king or prince
or knight.
above their kind
she wanted him be
their coo and smiles were satan's plot.
their gifts she insisted
were delilah's trick.

lo and behold when
he dare to choose his love
and hoped
she'd wish him best . . .
as such declared a friend
should fearlessly do . . .
she set out to conduct
a contest strange
in psychology
with warnings to derange.

his deal then done
and she surely knew
her hopes and dreams
are hers not his . . .
she had made for
him of what she wished his.

she called them friends
whom would his enemies
be and woe betide them
that show that they could install,
maintain and his favor grow.
the friend she'd been
took to wings and flew
into his enemies
and piranha's arms.

he call her friend
his sentiment sincere as
was his wont to be but
she denounced him
now the fraud as so revealed
all the bridges she made
were anchored in shallow clay.

For Legacy

i read your words with a recall that then,
as i know now, my child of five
possessed a passion
whose time would come
whose tool would be mightier than the gun,
no gun that launched him . . . his word . . . ,
but the day's weapon deadlier than yesteryear sword.

i read your words and felt your pain,
i imagine now as i wondered
then how you and they passed each day,
with nary a word so you
could sense the depth
of pain that I also did bear or the silent love
even as you experienced absence.

your pain, i understand.
i'd understand too, if this initiated search for a grain of salt.

i read your words and know
now as i should have then
the pain of the hurt i felt that wrought my absence
was but a sliver of that which yours and theirs must have been.

i read your words with a ken
of your courage to maintain that line
where sidle love and hate
that same line set for me by my act.
and i feel of the hurt that you felt.

i assuaged my pride and not be the father we know i should have been.

for many a time as i contemplate the long passed
monday morn as she watched me pack . . . she who accompanies you
on that trip from your wallet to your eye . . . even her giving that helping hand,
what different fate might we know had we eaten our pride,

for pride it was that let the one,
show the man i was and not the man we know i should have been,
the other to hide remorse for my hard cold bed instigated by her tat,
then foolishly answered with my destructive tit.

i read your words and want to convey
no desire or hope of forgiveness or understanding

but within dwells a deep penetration
of the depth of deprivation of firsthand experience which,
like the sands of time, remains suspended
in the ether, forever unknown.

a thank you sir, to the man I am proud to give respond.
a way to go, to the man i could emulate at his age . . .
next time around . . .
a thank you sire, and that's no pun to the father . . . !
hope i understood well
the existence of the child, because that's how

i read your words.

i read your words and attest
to their irrefutable validity
even as much as the sentiments i share,
having lived them and should have learned. yet the courage
to give life their expression gave me lecture
to dare examine and do repair ere my passing.

i read your words and as I caress
her bulging flesh where ensconced
our child i know now as i should have then
that i am the father we knew i must be.
for now manifest that part covered by the bushel
of legacy and pride and i-must-work-to-pay-the-bills hell
and not-enough-time excuses when being the father we
know i should have been has
matured into the father i am.

the father i know now to be that i was not
not the absence that the word conveyed to you.

i read your eloquence and my prayer . . . the one you prayed . . . ,
and wished for your own has been answered.
i know i am the father for her as we know
i should have been for you and for them.

nor absence.

i read your name
and know the score
and hope you can tell our pain one day,
to remain no more.

I Cease to Feel

I'm missing something
And I know not what
It is. But it's such a thing
No store has got
Or I'd quickly hie
To the vault and get
Wherewith to buy
The thing that I have not.

I'm missing something
And I know not what
It is. Not a cherished ring
As I've already gone
And done that deed
And if I had not
Would plan, indeed,
To sooner get it done.

I'm missing something
And I know not what
It is. Seemed the bling
Should curb the rot
Of lonely nights
And tossing, wrought
When alone, before,
Conspired I and done the plot.

I'm missing something
And I know not what
It is. For the nest still
Carries a void, not replete
With warmth and sound

Where, thought I,
The vow "I will"
Would a treasure complete.

I'm missing something
And I know not what
It is. The sleep then missed
Before the deed
Now pales … as oft

The nights I guard,
Bidding the warmth and sound
I craved, to materialize.

I'm missing something
And I know not what
It is. For freedom to go
As that to come
Do seem so far removed.
As the days ere the vows
Were read, beget
Urges of the going to come

I'm missing something
And I know not what
It is. The thought to go
Is easily sensed.
Yet, for the truth to flow
I first must admit,
The thought to go
Leaves my body tensed.

I'm missing something
And I know not what
It is. The courage for
Demise lies on the shelf.
Which is to say
Wrap those sentiments
In muslin gauze
I already have lost myself.

I'm missing something
And I know … "Heartache,
That's what." My going's a done deed.
So one and all hear the deal.
If the loss of oneself
Leaves flesh feeling numb,
Then hearts with long ache
Cease to feel.

Midnight Madness

They stayed awake
Counting time and words
Each as fast as was the other.
They counted the pain,
Recounted who hurt whom
As if one should win.

The silence cracked
As the pendulum swung,
Bringing chiming hands
In a vertical stand.
Still, no conclusion
Nor who should win.

The gray day passed
As did that last light;
The words she wrought,
The outsider's wand,
Strangely declared
That she did win.

Into the new darkness
As resolves harden
And diverse sides taken
'Tis clear by the gulf
In understandings and space
There is only a win
If reconciliations begin!

Night

You come so soon 'twas just first light
Seems it's now I should take noon's bite
Neither count sparse rays of beloved sun
Nor silent sheep of imagination's run.

You come too soon you forced time's hands
To traverse the face as your magic wand
Can only wish to slow the bell
That summons your darkness and your hell.

You come too soon they need to play
The youthful kin that count their day
In hours of mirth and stories said
Ere mom stern cry "It's time for bed."

You come too soon and you should know
You've lived and spent your to and fro
Whilst they who need their soul to keep
Face life and debt with dearth of sleep.

You come too soon I've yet to go
To see the maiden I enamor so
For as her day be opposed to mine
A machine I must for time design
You come too soon the dream I need
To tame and wear is here indeed
But just like scores I lived before
Will arouse me ere she nears my door.

On Moving On

Call him selfish
She did!
She erred!
That is his gift,
His being kind, undeterred.
Seems what his answer
Confirmed, confirmed
That he has forever
Gone to another place;
Having moved on
To where her heart
Will be free, unfettered.

As so also should his.

These years he understood
Unbound,
on this their planet,
Free to follow
their chosen path.
Yet,
wasn't it the same
Selfish he that gave
The ask of her unselfish
Spirit
if that were the
Result she wished to achieve?

The answer
she variously gave
They now manifest: apart.
The question then brought
The hurt that he dreaded most.

And, the result wrought
But kept unasked, would
Make believe there were
Hopes though actions
Did show otherwise.

Now, today,
New beginnings nigh
And sadness at neap.
Such tide of hate, methinks;
And forgetfulness
of the past
Let the words that were
her wont: "you are selfish"
Find again, their place.

Dishonestly at the fore
He understands.
He forgives but
He disavows.

Question of Friendship

what, on this day, could make
one friend speak evil to the other
when the need for help lurked
ominously at one's front door?
can it be that my thought
of friendship is too rigid and
needs adjusting?

or is it others'
that needs massaging!
It should mean, by me,
that there's no hurt to hurl,
no hurt to shag,
no dagger to thrust
molded by an urgent
need one cannot fulfill.

should not a friend be kind
in the expression of a need
to soothe, whose delivery,
by previous implied pact should
be yet many days away,
but now demanded suddenly?

lets me wonder the precept of friendship.

does it serve only to whet one's wont
to ask and receive and not
to give and understand,
to pay the price,
to reciprocate or heed
the golden rule?

Survival is Selfish

is it just he who feels
the pangs
of loneliness
and walk the paths,
at night, of cold
longing to nowhere?

is it just he who knows
this trek
for nowhere
does naught to quench
the thirst for touch or
consummate balm for
turgid flesh and
swollen mind?

is it just he who fears
the days
that turn
to months can churn
the pits, can do their pitting
on the innermost matrix
of the being? if so,
let him stand alone.

alone forsaken and
isolate
by the hordes
of they who do battle
in mind, in body,
in sinews; who know his
journey to the ken;
who turned their backs ere the
light of weakness shines brightest
on a plateau
of beckoning relief.

for of this, as selfish,
he's accused.

that mind and body
and core itself
heed their imperative,
to him remain just.

if tender plea
and urge
of warm embrace
can spark no urge
for her to communicate,
then the act to assuage
and placate
his need for endocrine
poise be just.

this, accomplished when
mind and body
be bloated by the poison
of life's deceit
or by survival's own
imperative is just.

if he be alone and,
imbued of this state,
capitulates, when the
urge to be as designed
heeds what his sanity,
can't dismiss; then,
be it known, selfish be right.

the urge for flourish
and survival be above
the urge to conform,
when to conform is
to succumb and lie extinct.

Storm

the storm came
suddenly,
powerfully.
breaking all
in its path.

and silence.
face strained
with indelible
grimace as
tracers and bullets
flew from the
gaping face.

relieved
was she.

the ruins left
by the storm
were, simply,
of words
that shattered
not only hers
but
his calm.

Troubled

she left his sight
and went, last night,
prostrate in bed
making a tiny ripple in
a flimsy linen engulfing
the body. a hum of
the machine is barely
felt yet its effect is plain.
the heavy blanket is
flung across her core.
he can hear her words,
not said this time, "i am
cold," tho' still full clad.
somnolent eyes, droopy, draws
him close as he knows
the end is there. past days
layers of garb belie their
pact of yester time. sidled
up did he to bare her body
but her protest caught
him aback, as did her
promise … "she won't sleep
yet." one night thence
he, all alone, her sauce
on him then served,
now relived,
lay sleepless and perplexed.
she is asleep in the minute
still clad … a barrier erect did
say not then, not him,
just her. makes him recall
a vow once made, oft kept,
that deeds he would when
senses dictate, not their
time of people who summon
him for theirs. the die is cast.
he, scared by new creativity, writes.
he writes when sad, disquieted.
writes he when perturbed.
which writings tell every time of
the spirit, troubled.

The Gander, the Goose

When he requested of
Her a massage for his
Aching shoulder,
The reply he got started him
It embarrassed
So much that he
Got a chill across the
Only part of him not
Overly sensitive on that
Day . . . his heart.
For it was the same
Outstanding ache that
Remained untouched from
That day's requests.
Her answer, then, was
Encoded as a clever joke.
"Get rid of the shoulder," she told,
"And the ache would go."
Now, today, the answer
Did not echo as a joke.
Even as he ask again while
Reviewing his play, but resonates
In his heart, in his very
Soul. It came a quick retort.
"Get your solitaire to do it!"
Oh, he thought, dismayed
Only he plays solitaire as she
Did go off to sleep. Then
For amusing himself
Only ever so quietly
Resigned he to employ
That game that needed not
Her company.
Or another's
Even if lonely he got.
Good then that he can
On the next event that she
Only needs a massage of wherever
Should reply in like fashion
"Employ your 'Klondike' for the job!"
But he will not use a tit for a tat.

They Called Your Name

ten years ago today
the townsfolk called you pris;
though I was named priscilla and you,
my sister, chris.

ten years ago today
if you should get a toy,
you'd look at me and say
hi there little sister
i want to give you this!

ten years ago today
the war and call up came and
when i picked my number you
let them call your name.

ten years ago today
you proudly told me then, war is just not for you,
pris you're better with a pen.

ten years ago today
as we stormed into iraq you
went and did my duty you
were my shield and rock.

ten years ago today you
let me miss the fight
went and defend our country
you said it was alright.

ten years ago today
seemed you knew so well
as you filled the backpack
that you would hear your knell.

I had not then an inkling don't
know how you could tell,

but
ten years ago today this
I remember well.

ten years ago today
your cherished wand you gave;
asking me with much fervor to
"put this in my grave."

ten years ago today your love
for me displayed when you just
took my number
and then they wrote your name.

Fall to Spring

(Also titled Around Christmas)

Lawn mower drained and put away,
Rake and hose and nozzle in stow
Firewood stacked and waiting,
The fill of fireplace and hearth to glow.
Grass has been treated for autumn's ride
Plants pruned and culled and blanketed,
Trees gave their colorful leaves for mulch
Lone dandelion stymied and wilted.

Christmas lights, stockings, and decorations
From dungeons' guts released,
Tree used year over year for savings
Makes hugger and me quite pleased.
And as treasures 'neath its lush are chosen
Receivers' faces alight with glee,
Brackish ponds now flat and frozen
Invite the sleighs and skaters free.

Dripping icicles give the news
Of cold fronts' and snows' retreat
Birds' new songs and wings aflutter
Bear fact of springtime treats.
Lawn begins to show its life
And day's rays and warmth resume
Once lonely wilted dandelion
Grows resplendent in yellow plume.

When Love Dies

those years it was love,
not now.

all the happy times then,
were to his benefit;
she made them happy.
today he is the source of their sad.

the sun shone
only on his
side of the road
they traversed.

the music played on the far side
without rhythm, save when she drove.

those wonderful gourmet eats
he enjoyed,
while she watched.

the gifts then shared are now hers,
any returned are parceled to her.
benefits derived
accrued to him
as were cuddles and warmth.
and grin.

twenty five he remained,
the age when they met,
the time they spent
add twenty years to her ledger . . .
those ten years together.

'twas a bad dream she had
but she aged through that nightmare
as her time he took,
and his eluded the book.

the times of togetherness
were for his pleasure,
the joys of love
he received
as she looked.

now
he knows it is regrettable
they met,
though friends saw that
she was his pet.

the offspring they bore
are her safety net.
to see them
has he permission to get.

she lets them keep his
name just as she keeps
the chattels
and the jewelry and
lucre he may earn.

the worse person now in
the land a deadbeats:
then, he was
drop dead a beau.

that was then.

Mystery of Sleep

I watched you sleep:
watched you with morning eyes,
as the street below,
and I awakened;
whether it by me or
I by the warmth of your skin.

the lines of your face!
parallels by eyes and lips
punctuated the circular orifices . . .
guides for the channels
of sustaining life force.

such angelic quiet of
your countenance
and
your breathing exchanges,
belie the thunderous
din
of hours past,
ere I capitulated to the urge to sleep.

Lets me ponder the mystery
that drives the difference
between this manifest calm
and the reveling,
which partners daily
your every punch line . . .
just as the wonder of the
mystery sandwiched
between
your jaded goodnights
and your
cheerful energetic
good mornings.

Twinkle Twinkle

"twinkle twinkle little star
how I wonder what you are"
learned that as a child did she.
stars twinkled in the dark
of the rustic backwardness
when the moon did not
come out to play.
but she did,
her siblings and she.
stars not only
twinkled but paraded in different
sizes as each tried to outdo
the others in brightness,
size and color. what are they really,
was her wonder. now she knows
as she watched mr. jeweler
polish her grandma's
old gold and silver baubles.
this, along with the plethora
of signs she passed
with her nose pressed
firmly against the car window
in city traffic. congested traffic
giving time to study the sights
while visiting her aunt in the city.
toronto has answered the thought
how I wonder what you are
this is her learning experience.
her mind overflowed with knowing
what with all these signs
offering cash for gold cash for silver,
cash for old jewelry. she can
only imagine that somehow
all this gold and silver would,
having been turned to dust,
eventually be taken way above
in a gas balloons by
jewelers aides at night,
and sprinkled in the skies
way up above while yonder
sun from across the sphere
shines its light on the gold
and silver dust reflecting
the light in its many different colors.
twinkle twinkle little star
no more wonder what you are.

Waves, Our Time

they keep rolling by,
the waves, knowing not
what they are or whence
they came who sent them
and why.
but daily
without surrender
thought or pause
traverse a course
which, unknown to them
hitherto prescribed,
draws them ever
so slowly, so silently, so powerfully,
to our land. ultimately,
like so invisible a ghost,
through the heavens
into a fleeting universe
not ever mindful,
they must return,
reincarnated in form,
to resume a never-ending trek,
a quest even, to find the
why of their existence,
how they originate,
where they go,
for whom they came,
how they, as they caress
our sandy, rocky, marshy shores,
screech to a sudden violent death.
but we must know, each,
respectively, is our time rolled by
never to be reclaimed f
rom the heavens
through which we are taken,
guided by our own devices
through the same unyielding force
of their existence.

OBSERVATIONS

Cars

The scene from my office window
On fifth-floor southern glow
Provides the perfect setting
To contemplate their to and fro.
Cars aplenty, east and west
Along four-o-one corridor;
I watched and counted many cars,
Violating the highway laws.

Blue cars, white cars, cars with paint aglow.
Sleek cars, thick cars, cars with tires for snow.
Dull cars, pretty cars, cars with Jack and Jills.
Cars I like, cars I hate, cars with all the frills.
Cars with scars and cars carrying goods.
Cars with emblems on their hoods.
I watched and counted many cars
With scars from earlier wars.

Mean cars, serene cars, cars with cats and dogs.
Slow cars, fast cars, cars with young road hogs.
Braking cars, screeching cars, straddling the lanes.
Crashing cars, volatile cars, enveloped in flames.
Men in red tanks came for the wetting
As I watched from the perfect setting
On fifth-floor southern glow
The scene from my office window.

Coco Malibu

pop!
malibu
mr. walker
sneaked into the gathering
last friday eve
as the setting sun
left the fatigue of
the last six
upon their shoulders.

one, two, three, four.
bottoms up.
no . . . !
down the hatch.

savor coconut and
rum and smiles and
slurs and words not
dared spoken
without the help
of coco malibu.

tomorrow she
works and she.
but she takes
another, she also.

more talk and more
laughter and
surprises.

the door to renal
and hepatic relief
goes ajar.

fluid sounds drown
complete awareness
of midnight
and next day's labor.

of love,
no mention.
of work,
dimension belies
the late scene.

pop?
no . . . !
malibu. and punch of rum
"down the hatch"
hi rum!
no pop.

December Treats

many years past
the ground would
greet me with a blanket
so white the eyes
squinted to accept
its presence with the sun.

the wind bit hard as ploughs
assembled as if for battle.

roads sat treacherous
tires froze and trundle
to banks of snow so hard
that metal would crumble
at their contact. thirty
years hence the
late december grass
is green, the ground
shun a white garb
mostly loving the
calm and warmer days
fashioned from
our lifestyles.

some may say that this
was inevitable as man
bade beasts and birds
and fishes and bees
follow their evolved
need to thaw the air.

that once so surely at this
time of year brought the
gifts of snow and salt and
sleet and slush and lack
of heat
just as surely as Santa's
elves delivered their treats.

Day to Day

Morning dew, hanging mist
Feathery bliss of dawn's first kiss.
Fire yonder east, new day to ponder
Past night's deep slumber.

No dream to remember.

First dark brew
Of natures bud.
The ancient ban
A resounding thud.

Fumes and fumers
Booms and boomers.
Trucks and truckers
And tricks and tricksters.

Friends and foe
Leaders in woe
Finicky machines
News and magazines
Selling wares
And denouncing fears
Of economic gloom
And impending doom.

With bears and bulls
And puts and pulls
Same sex and no sex

And heads and shoulders sorely vex
By workload and download
Front load and no load
Warrants and warranties.

Political parties
Right and Left
And right to life
Toke and tokens and strike and strife.

Plays of Thespians
And Gays and lesbians.
Age of consent
And morality descent.
Toils gone sour
To last rush hour.
Rush home last prance
Home sides' last chance.

First nap, last wine
Nightcaps, supine till the chime
Beckons the new
Morning dew, hanging mist
Feathery bliss of dawn's first kiss.

I Hate Hamburgers

the words you hear from
january to april are

. . . tax time . . .

makes one think, wrongly,
that those are the only months
that we pay taxes.

people gather
evidence of earnings,
evidence of expenses
lest they fall behind and
incur other penalties,

that is, simply,
pay more taxes.

i have not heard
of anyone who likes to pay taxes none
that would like to pay more taxes

except paul.
my friend paul.

he fervently contends
his desire is to pay more taxes,
taxes in the multimillions.
fifty million.

that's fifty million dollars . . . per year.

that, then,
would be his boast.

we all, says he,
really do love to pay taxes.
just not wish to
talk about it.

except for income tax,
and property tax and sales tax.
taxes we talk about
january to april

not one word of
breakfast tax,
lunch tax,

tax on buns,
tax on butter.

tax on

beef, tax on cheese, tax on tomato,
tax on mayonnaise, tax on onions,

tax on ketchup, tax on pickles,
tax on mustard, tax on relish.

but we leave home and
gladly order hamburger

then we stretch our
mouths gaping wide,
like moby dick open wide,
to stuff all that
taxes down our gullets.

don't you hate hamburgers?

i hate hamburgers.

Kiss of Tears

zinnias in full bloom!
he stymied the boiling
midafternoon tropical heat, cultivating,
mulching, caressing the ground
for moist roots of his
treasured flowered friends.
already quenched in
the early morning,
just after sunup, they paraded thick
dark-green garb which, today,
would seem artificial,
forty years later.

the cool of the under bush
belie the furnace that baked
the apices of pink, beauteous
crowns, like advantaged queens
in a rustic setting. the robust howl
of produce truck a hundred meters
north compromised the silence . . .
silence that exposed an undeclared
yet practical siesta, compelled
by the languish instilling heat
of the jamaican summer.

the wind, or lack thereof,
is detected only by the space
between the long departed truck,
the remnant of its passing melody
now only a faint hypnotic hum
way in the distance, and the
intoxicating sulphurous essence
of its exhaust fumes.

It was this scene, this memory that
he relived as he drove his vehicle
of employment, bus number seven thousand
one hundred fourteen, westward along
eglinton to jane from weston. so potent
was this memory of zinnia, country lorry,
aromatic waste of spent sulphur . . .
and silence that the tears
drowning from the corners
of the eyes were a betrayal of
emotions that enveloped him
forty years after the scene.

Locusts

They came from the east
They came for the feast
The pests
The locusts.
They swarm
They harm
They came a cloud
An aerial flood
The pests
The locusts.
Their mindless plan.
They swarm
The crops in the field.
They wield
Their devastations
On our cultivations.
They came
They swarm
They harm
They had their feasts.
The beasts gave up there
As the pests laid bare
Then flew west.
The crops, too, succumb
And none will come
To maturity.
No pan did clang
No smoke did provoke
Their mindless plan.
The locusts
The pests
An aerial flood.
They came a cloud
They harm
They swarm.
The locusts
The pests
They came for the feast
They came from the east.

Mr. Wind

hello, mr. wind!
most people
believe
you can never be seen
and i believe
that too. really!

i know when you are here, though.
you do not hide
yourself very well.

it seems,
too, that you are either
very wide
or very long,
the same.

you are mostly
calm and weak
but can be provoked to strength.
you may wonder
how I know this . . .

. . . when you visit
our space
you impart so much energy
to everything.

sometimes you tarry
deliberate
in carrying out your will.
push with unerring
accord from one
direction:
always the same.

you sometimes
come from the east
and sometimes
from the west,
sometimes from the north
and sometimes
from the south.
people in town

make beautiful
songs about you.
sometimes they hate you.

mostly, they like you
when you are peaceful and warm,
nice and slow.

then, they hate you
when you are cold,
with your
freezing chill on
a winter's day.

some I know always pretend
that you are not there
but methinks
they can feel your presence.
they resist the temptation to
show how much
they are affected by you
sometimes
to their detriment.

one tall structure in my city,
which, for a time
was the tallest freestanding
structure on the planet,
cannot help but show its
welcome for your presence.

it simply waves
back and forth each
way three or more feet.

back and forth she swings
but gradually reduces intensity
reflecting your passage;
reduce her swing as you
reduce your power
over her.
i also notice that
you visited me at
home today.

You seem to have
no effect on my house but
I could tell you were there.
see!
mr. gutter rebelled
as you tried to relieve
him of mr. eaves,
and good old mr. elm made
so much protest
as you pushed him
to the ground.

can't you understand
and admit
that even three-year-old
tommy knew that
you pushed
mr. elm over?

did he stand in your way?

he was there before you
many years before!

the leaves you dislodged
from their arboreal
lodgings
what wrong did they do you?
why did you pick
some and not others?

did they have to be governed
by your will?
having them go
the same direction as you?

whatever the reason
i can tell your visit,
that is the main point.

sometimes, though,
you are pleasant
sometimes you are
from the pot.
sometimes you have
calm disposition
sometimes you

are fiery hot.
sometimes you're a
storm with a name
(made my sister cry that
you took her name,
poor hattie, i wiped her tear)
a zephyr sometimes.

you cry too,
and sometimes
you bring sad and grey
sometimes you show calm
and let the children play.

mostly, though, mr. wind,
i love you best
when you come to remove
the wet from my chest the
tears from my eye
or let the clouds
flow from the sky
like a sweet
by-and-by.

mr. wind,
you let me unwind
when you are calm
you make me wonder
whence you came
and how you go.

mostly
you make me ponder
that without your to and fro,
there'd be no snow
there'd be no rain,
there'd be
no grain
and no sow
and no reap.

come again, mr. wind.
i'll wait you till spring.

and for you
i shall sing.

Sign of the Times

winter's wrath did
naught to cool the
vengeance
that stole her heart.

to think that those
same beat
did drum
of caring and sharing
till the end.

those vows
broken
are fled to the ether,
forgotten.
he must be punished
as no perished vows ever before.

hers?
what promise?
his sacrifices are but
thoughts so to
act upon
if her spirit so
decides or does her mother's.

'twas done
in the winters
cold when torments not felt
as the purr of man
and machine
became
the sole sound of
the white expanse,
and sleep came
'neath ice encrusted branches.

but two decades and
some passed whilst faded
feelings with words, worried
of half-truths or none,
give meanings to
mean and vengeful,

even as deed
for guilt
were life's support.

or
that a molding of
devilish device to
breed the act, had
simply matured to give
proof or its appearance
that the deeds and
her hurt were real.

that they were not culmination
of a deep dormant desire
for permanent change.

the change that ultimately came.

Ode to Spring

White fields now turned to green
Soggy underfoot gone firm
As buds and blooms and twits and tits
Turn men from stupor to their wits.

Rested sun regains a wont to shine
Thoroughfares do their ebon smile
As pylons and posts and yonder spire
Project their pristine new attire

The westerly winds have lost their bite
Flurries and slush vanish from sight.
Clocks and roosters advance their crow
And tears of winter spurned do slow.

Frocks and shorts replace thick coats
Sandals and pumps do boots
And forms and figures change the scene
Once drab and cold sans facial sheen

See how once sere crabgrass now thrive
Wasps and bees work hard in hives
Reds and yellows of petals bow
To aromas of lime and thyme and chives.

Celebrate the birds this time of glee
Of Cardinals, Blue Jays and Orioles free
Contracts renewed and sliders wing
Memories of Tom say ode to spring.

Payday Blues

how slowly
this filthy lucre from
two weeks' sweat
travels on official
corporate paper,
through the maze
meticulously conspired
upon us by
the equally filthy banks
holding gluefully
with such debilitating claws
as the compulsory
seven days pass!

their devices sanctioned
by the high foreheads
of the land, allow our bread
to only trundle along
the snail of a monetary
circuit for their benefit.

then, lo and behold,
cash is available
but, for the millisecond it is so,
also are the hooks activated . . .
those preauthorized crooks.

they get their equally evil
sticky fingers on the dough
ere it could cool in the ovens
of those cavernous vaults.
methinks i wait for the
next and hope my need
for sustenance be less
than their rapacious
need of my pay.

Tears of Love

If you cannot cry
you know not
the path that tears travel
along the winding road
to the world,
that it starts in the
heart out of fear or
out of joy, out of happiness,
or out of longing, out of pride or out of pain,
out of sadness or out of loneliness.

Or out of revenge!

Out of bitter unfulfilling revenge!

The load, the weight descents
upon the heart, the lungs the forehead,
the brain the loins.

And sleep
is like a ton of bricks
settling slowly on the flesh
the mind and the dream,
while you despise
the thousands of sheep.

Maybe you fight, resist,
breathe deeply, clench
the flesh between the teeth,
and think of the clouds as
chariot for the object of your pain,
loneliness, and
longing; the journey ending
at the doorstep to the heart.

Yet the ache never goes
and the hot and tired
thirst yearn for the dewdrops
that thins the acid,
the ache, the anger, even,
and the soothe of pain.

But it doesn't rain.

If there is success to deny
the rain for these seeds
there is failure to provide
that balm for the night, the fight,
the ache which must reside
if there is love.

And there is love, undoubtedly.

Or where from come fear,
joy happiness, longing pride,
pain, sadness, loneliness, and a heavy heart?

All children of love!

And jealousy!

All precursors of the
briny express of poison that
fails to dull the ache
and pain and sadness.

They dwell with you then
leave a sense of hope that
the body be replenished to
welcome the next episode.

(what next episode?
i am now strong
and impervious to it all.
there is no rewind
or repeat or desire for repeat
so what next episode?)

Brings the thought to bear
if you cannot cry,
you cannot love.

Winter's Lament

but a few chilly winters past
the blizzards' bite did last
all day and night.
and months again!

i'd long to see the rain

the sun would shine.
the usual brine
by road treat and yonder sun
did not materialize deferred
by frozen cold.

mountainous cakes of snow
piled head high
along the thoroughfare
became iced
with salt and sand.

see city hall women and men
with tall foreheads debating
cost in dough and
time to plough?

reaching there from here,
would take a year
but you'd need to find
a taxi man who's kind.

the snow came today
following the countdown
and happy new year.

a week passed:
the cold next.

i did think it odd
they all were vexed..
who expected the clime,
wrought, no doubt
by their own deeds,
to hide winters depth
and breadth; when
but a few chilly winters past
the chills arrived
ere the frills, lights, carols,
and frost seduced their sills

Wisteria

Aster, Althea, Amaryllis,
Azalea, Angelica, and Armeria.
Achillea, Arnica, Astelia,
Abelia, Acaena, and Begonia
Blossom and Barkenia.
Cerinthe, Cistanthe,
Cleome, and Camellia.
Dalia, Daffodil, Daisy Dill,
and Delphinium.
Erica, Freesia, and Felicia.
Gardenia, Godetia,
and Gilly Hyacinth and Honesty.
Iris, Jade, and Jasmine.
Jacinth and Jamaica.
Katsura and Lily and
Lilac Lavender and Melissa.
Magnolia, Marigold,
Nandina, Neillia,
Nerine Nicandra, and Nolana.
Orchid, Peony,
Poppy Pansy, Petunia, Primrose.
Queen and Rose, Rosemary
Roselle, and Salvia.
Thalia, Tulip,
Tilia Ume, and Umeko.
Violet, Wisteria Xenia,
Xigua, Xyris Yasmin, and Zinnia.
All with a common link.
All flowers, all ladies,
Unless, of course, you say
"Mr. Rose!"

SOCIAL

Africa

The land of the free
Free people, free range
People free to be taken
Free to be taken . . . enslaved.
Free for bloodshed.

So many of our people made dead.

The land of the free
Free to toil, free to boil
In the burning sun
Free to be freed
Freed, with a burning pride.
Our people from apartheid.
The land of the free
Free to be raped and plundered
Free to be lied to, lied about
Free to be hated
Free to be scorched.
Against our people debauched.

The land of the free
Now more free
Free to talk back
Free to fight back
Free to avenge.

For our people take revenge.

Lands of the free
We all must agree.
Must make free
Dar . . . free Darfur!
Free Africa . . .
Free your guilt.

Your worlds our Africa built!

Eliminate Stress

to eliminate stress
and help
happiness to grow,
you need to
eliminate hate,
put a stop to worry,
give more while
expecting less;
live simply,
love generously,
care deeply,
speak kindly,
and leave the rest
to the universe.

Apple Dish

apple cake, apple pie, dried apple,
applesauce, apple turnover, fried apple;
apple chutney, apple juice, apple betty,
apple skillet, apple salsa, apple butter.

apples for baking, apples for stewing, red apples,
apples for juicing, apples for spicing, green apples;
gala apples, fuji apples, apples for cheese and wine,
pink lady, golden delicious, apples to sieve very fine.

apple juice, apple cobbler, spiced apple,
apple squares, apple coolers, diced apple;
apple crisp, apple slice, apple conserve;
apple waffle, apple marmalade preserve.

spartan, adanac, ambrosia, and arlies red,
granny smith, arcane, rosette, and albany beauty;
of over seven thousand varieties in the book,
which apple dish would you like me to cook?

Friendly Advice

Be strong today and recognize
the dignity of work. Challenge yourself
to live by a strict percent rule,
putting aside that fraction of your earnings
day for day as a pie for the future.
Do that without fail for you will fail
to become more prosperous
if you neglect this. Do so religiously.
As well, think not of those who seek
to do harm nor of their devices.
But be proud of who you are, what you are,
and what you do. Laugh in their faces
by always wearing a smile and positive attitude.
Never forget those who care the most for you.
Rather, do the same for them not because
they seek it but because they deserve it.
Remember, always, that your thought
of the reason one does any deed against you is just
one thought of millions of possibilities.
Even the wisest is apt to be wrong in this regard.
Besides, it is counterproductive. You
gain more if you think of the reasons things go well.
It is always because you did what was necessary for
them to go well. Listen well if you want to learn.
Speak about others only if you have something edifying to impart.
Pay attention to the words of your friends but
be extra-attentive to those of your enemies. For
theirs can have the greater impact on your life.
Do good for everyone. Let those deeds be spoken of
only by others if they care to speak them. Enjoy what you do each
day for it will make your days short and your life long.
Accept the blessings of your achievements
and possessions and share with the less fortunate,
not the unwilling. Do well today
in all you attempt, for it sets a precedence for
action as you begin the rest of your life.

Gillian

I listened to her, thirteen,
As she played a ditty gay;
Thought of the babe they handed me
That wondrous day that May

I saw the eyes that questioned
The place now new and bright;
Yet ne'er a thought of danger
Crossed her face nor of fright

Her arms were smooth and slender,
Her legs portend of speed,
Her gaze, first firm, did wander
From side to side indeed.

I heard the sound that signaled
Apgar for which to be proud;
Her pupils told me then and there
"Je sais vous etes mon pere!"

I saw report cards come that show
Results that speak of gold;
Siblings' rivalry, the best I know,
Were never slow to unfold.

The guitar, the pool, track, and tact,
Gymnastics and injuries and act;
The laughter and tears are just as sweet
As jamoca almond fudge for treat.

That soothing voice reveals her charm
Her heart can do no harm;
For friend and foe alike do know
It's empathy and care that show.

"Good night, Dad" can never bring
A better feel to a king;
And the next day as the sun does rise,
The glint's stuck in her eyes.

If

If you can make new friends while keeping
The faithful old as on life's journey, you progress;
Take new advice while not forgetting
The old that got you on the path to success;
If you give thanks to the new yet not discount
Those that you gave on many a day,
When first you sought and gain the trust,
That helped put to substance for which you did pray:

If you can accept new bounties offered freely
Of those who seem to be the savior,
And not despise the now modest and needy,
Nor share disdain for first gift and favor;
If you can count the blessings of the evening,
And not forget the mornings that gave the start,
To keep the flame of passion burning
While holding only to the godly heart:

If you can recall the hurt and injury
As gratitude to you then overdue,
Was held, instead replaced with slight
And which your tears gave force to subdue;
If you can grow and keep your roots
Not turning hard nor giving full prize,
That once was shared as once was earned
But now seem spent for their surprise:

If you can still keep true to your heart
And your maker's law be followed without fear;
If all of these you reconcile only in part
Or not fail to recount the facts from the start;
If you and yours can welcome sleep
And not at the start need the count of sheep
You will find in the end your acts be unwise,
If the new who courted, now made your demise.

New Year's Blessing

they once parted ways
he to wilson.

she stayed put
in the nest they had built
on bathurst,
where they then
and now
call home.

she, calm seemingly
not easily ruffled, sits there
enjoying the crowd totaling
twenty then some,
in between dozes.

he,
just centimeters
above in stature,
and gregarious,
loves to dance;
loves the
tipple somewhat.
teaches
the steps to one
young guest.

one contemplating
or
surveying the scene
would not fail
to note it consists
mostly of dames . . .
young, not
so young, single,
married with children.

some sleep while
the reveling.
karaoke, as usual,
and game-dancing.

paper dance,
potato dance,
hospital and buzz.

champagne came in foams.

the new year went in blinks;
some depart
and play continues.

the main context, though,
of this repast and games
remain the kindness
and charm
of him and her no more parted,
to invite, to provide,
to entertain,
to give of their modest means.

count not the venue
nor count the cost in
time or ample repast.

but count their smiles
and count their joy,
count their togetherness.

the alarm activated
by sparklers of new year's
celebration or chance that
the neighbors, above or below
could complain,
cannot dampen the spirit
of the kindness from this pair
and their beloved child.

instead
count the blessing to accrue
one for which this impressed
found-in has just prayed.

Practical Advice

Be strong today
and recognize
the dignity of work.

Challenge yourself
to live by a strict percent rule,
putting aside that fraction
of your stipend
day for day as a pie
for the future.

Do that without fail
for you will fail
to become more prosperous
than if you neglect this.

Do so religiously.
as well, forget not those who
seek to do harm nor
their devices.

But, within the law,
do them back
fourfold.

Be proud of who you are
and laugh
in their faces.

Always think big
and possess a
positive attitude.

Never forget
those who care the
most for you.

Rather, do the same for them
not because they seek it
but because they deserve it.

Remember, always,
that the competition
will try to bury you.

They enjoy doing this
so it is your duty
to reciprocate.
Examine what works well for
you and improve it.
Listen well if you
want to learn
and edify those
who deserve it.

Never fail
to advertise those that
wrong you deliberately.

Pay attention
to the words of your
friends but
be extra-attentive
to those of your enemies
for theirs can have
the greater impact
on your life.

Do good
for everyone
but let those deeds of your
enemies precede them

enjoy what you do each day for it will make your
days short
and your life long.

Accept the blessings of your achievements and
possessions and
share with the less fortunate, not the unwilling.

Do well today
and spend, everyday, planned time
on the activity in which you wish to succeed.

Never give up on your dream for it is the
precedence
for action and success
for the rest of your life.

Precursors

if you hope for understanding
you must first
seek knowledge
if you hope to succeed
you must
expect to fail
if you hope to be satisfied
you must
know hunger and thirst
if you hope for forgiveness
you must
learn to forgive
if you hope for peace
you must
know the concept of war
if you hope to achieve
you must
first make the start
if you hope to stand tall
you must
get off our seat
if you hope to reach the stars
you must
begin to dream
if you hope to ever receive
you must
know to always give.

Reach for the Sky

Stretch arms for flexibility
And your legs to split well
Stretch imagination's ability,
As a child cast in a spell.
Stretch your lung to capacity
Get your full eight-ounce due
Stretch your openness for friendship
More than gold could soon accrue.
Stretch your search for knowledge
Your mental power to increase
Stretch your marks for great grades
Not unsightly tummy crease.
Stretch your lips or fistula
For adornment or for rite
Stretch your money at months' end
But remember to pay your tithe.
Stretch your thoughts through the ether
Its power to connect to
Him Stretch your capacity for greatness
Your diligence to aid your world.
Stretch your story or your truth
Make more interesting not the lie
Stretch for achievement and success
Set your reach for the sky.

Sabine

Eyes that bespeak of sincerity
As plots unfold and retold,
In brown and white they glisten bright
With focus as fine gold.

Pages consumed do tell a tale
Of changes that come with time,
For seems a couple moons just past
Her first would be her last line.

The laugh does echo far and wide
With strength and surfeit of fun,
The power derived from practice and use
Brings might to her every pun.

No dinner is as good or diner
As the homemade on friendly patio,
The wont to launder is only surpassed
By the shun of banana and tomato.

The journeys that begin at her bed
Take her far and wide in her sleep,
The facts told then unknown at dawn
Reveal no urge to count sheep.

No early morning tea for me
Just let the weekend begin,
This day the hours for sleeps a score
Being up before noon a sin.

Sabine does help the world go round
And round some heads will turn,
If friendship with Simone ever go
Ere our solar disc cease to burn.

She Walked Out My Door

Hello, morning!
Hello, sunshine!
Let me wait.
Let me wait till the shadows
That I cast
Are from above;
That the warmth that they bring
Are from my love
For she took her belongings and walk out my door
And I fear she ain't coming back no more.

Hello, midday!
Hello, dark fears!
Let me wait.
Let me wait till the evening
Brings me joy,
Allay my fears;
And the presence of long shadows
Dry my tears.
For she took her belongings and walked out my door
And I fear she ain't coming back no more.

Hello, evening!
Hello, twilight!
Let me wait.
Let me wait till the moonlight
And the silence
Of the night
Bring her home to my arms
Erase my fright.
For she took her belongings and walked out my door
And I fear she ain't coming back no more.

Hello, midnight!
Hello, dagger!
I can't wait.
I can't wait till the morning
Brings the sorrow
Back again
She, if lost, then for me
Let death be gain
As she took her belongings and walked out my door
Life for me ain't worth living anymore.

Tribute to Toronto

My, my, how she has grown
And history books have shown
This town has always been
Toronto the clean!
Once intimate Town of York Has
developed a spunk and spark
The world has come to know Toronto.
TO.

If by chance you leave T'ranna,
Come right back you know you're gonna,
For when you are feeling low
There's no place you rather go
Than Toronto; TO.

When it's my time to leave
This planet,
You better believe;
They'll put me underground,
W here I can always hear the sound,
Of Toronto
Toronto!
Toronto!
Toronto, TO

The Past Lives

time does not yield
or make
a change to
the sense that
past remain.
cannot
be undone
its fruits remain, indelible.
good fruits
or bad
happy
or sad must live
to keep the universe
in place.
change the reality
should make them
not be.
but, here they are.
together
result of their reality.
his reality
as time reveal.
so his past must abide;
concealment keeps it yet.
beats him, then, that
she should
make a stir . . . no
. . . an eruption
when
evidence of the path
to her
does
reveal itself. where then
should he
have traversed
to her so that
that reality
could bring them here
to where
they abide?

Westward

Two broke rancher's sons on the run
Thought they'd stop just a while for some fun
Ventured into booze store
Whiskey each then four more
But one started a play with his gun.

The mistaken ace shot of the town
Thought this bloke must sure be a clown
Put a shot in the air
Then bellowed to the pair
Leave town or I'll put you both down.

But the men on the run had no fear
They had taken the best far and near
Yet one remembered the chase
And thought "why win this case
And be roped should we not hurry clear?"

So grabbed he drunken kin by the arm
He who wanted to exhibit his charm
And hurried from the fight
Leaving the lady of the night
A date later will do him no harm.

He had escaped the posse this long
And their horses were yet very strong
So he thought it is best
If he continue his quest
To return to the town they belong.

The why of the chase he'd not known
But he thought he should go and be shown
He's a man in good standing
And the steer he'd been branding
Was culled from a ranch of his own.

He arrived at his town by and by
As the sun was adorning the sky
Good old Sheriff O'Grady
Had been briefed by his lady
That her sons would be hurrying nigh.

The young men arrived just in time
And the townsfolk, awakened by a chime
Bade the posse, "good-bye
Turn around, vanish, or die!
Leave our young men to enjoy their prime."

Zio Luigi

Suddenly, today,
my uncle passed away:
not really my uncle the
uncle of my partner.
she was distraught
and then we talked.
we talked about his
life the part we knew
his eighty-some years;
the smile he carried at
his son's cottage,
frank 's cottage,
at summertime.
his smile portrayed
good health . . .
his pink skin
shaven clean . . .
his eating well,
silently, peacefully.
we talked
about the dream . . .
my dream
last night

dream of my mother,
in the market
one aisle over.
she took my bag
insisting that she carry it.
we wondered about
the meaning
the meaning of dreams
the meaning of
dreams of the departed
the meaning of
this dream;
dream of my mother
who a decade ago today,
just like my uncle,
tio luigi,
the uncle of my partner,
suddenly, silently,
peacefully
passed away.

INDEX